Wreaths

for Every Season

24 Projects to Make Throughout the Year

Stasie McArthur

D1224443

Dover Publications, Inc.
Mineola, New York

Dedication

Thank you to CMM and KTM
for your constant love and support.

I am eternally grateful for the love and care that my project received from the Dover team. I would like to express my heartfelt appreciation to Terri Geus, Susan Rattiner, and Marie Zaczkiewicz for all of their great ideas and helpful suggestions. They helped with everything from editing, design, flushing out ideas, navigating potholes, and keeping me to task. Aside from being highly skilled at their jobs, they are amazing people. I wouldn't have been able to do this project without them, and I owe them more than these simple words for making this book a success. Thank you.

Photography: Roy Mauritsen
Location: courtesy of Urban Farmhouse, Bellmore, New York
Watercolor backgrounds: Getty Images

Bibliographical Note

Wreaths for Every Season: 24 Projects to Make Throughout the Year
is a new work, first published by Dover Publications, Inc., in 2020.

Library of Congress Cataloging-in-Publication Data

Names: McArthur, Stasie, author.
Title: Wreaths for every season: 24 projects to make throughout the year /
    Stasie McArthur.
Description: Mineola: Dover Publications, Inc., [2020]
Identifiers: LCCN 2019054695 | ISBN 9780486837444 (paperback)
Subjects: LCSH: Wreaths.
Classification: LCC TT899.75 .M33 2020 | DDC 745.92/6—dc23
LC record available at https://lccn.loc.gov/2019054695

Manufactured in the United States by LSC Communications
83744001
www.doverpublications.com

2 4 6 8 10 9 7 5 3 1
2020

Wreaths

for Every Season

Projects

Projects

Introduction

HOME DECOR can be expensive. I am excited to show you that it doesn't have to be, even if you have expensive tastes. Wreaths can be a simple, yet interesting way to accessorize your living space and show your unique style. Wreaths can be used on your exterior door to welcome friends and family to your home. You can also use wreaths inside your space, as wall hangings, or to accent mirrors, walls, and mantles.

I promise that you don't need to be super crafty to make the projects in this book. I will walk you through all of the steps needed to make unique pieces for your home, or to give as gifts. In addition to items you can buy online and at your nearest craft store or thrift shop, you will be surprised what you can create by upcycling or recycling what you already have on hand to create a wreath or embellish one.

With very basic supplies and a little bit of imagination, you will be able to create something for every season—and for special occasions like birthdays and weddings, you name it! These wreaths will look like you bought them at the hottest boutique or home decor store, but for a fraction of what you might have paid in those shops.

Much of my craftiness is just thriftiness, channeled in a different way. I know that I can always figure out how to replicate something I have seen in a store, and, many times, it's more cost-effective. It is awesome to be able to truly personalize your home decor items. Be inspired to put your own spin on these projects by using your favorite flowers or a color scheme that ties in perfectly with your space.

This is how I got started making wreaths . . . we were on vacation and stepped into a fabulous little boutique where I saw a wreath that I JUST HAD TO HAVE, but the price tag stopped me in my tracks. My hubby said I know you can make that and it would be nicer. Challenge accepted!

Inspiration

INSPIRATION is everywhere, so be open and receptive. Find a cataloging method that works for you so that you will always have a source of inspiration when you need it. I've created a few different boards within my Pinterest account, but I also have a simple binder with clear sleeves where I have everything from paint swatches to magazine pages to scraps of fabric, which is useful for quickly checking color combinations, or textures, or themes. You'll find you can get a lot of ideas by looking at your inspiration pieces when you are busy and have limited time to craft, or when you're stumped and need a starting point to get your creative juices flowing. I am a very visual and tactile person, so the fabrics and paint swatches work well for me, but this is something that should be personal to you. Take some time and figure out what inspires you.

Always use the best supplies and tools that you can afford, because they will give you the best chance of a successful outcome, in this case, beautiful wreaths and decor items! Don't rule out dollar stores and thrift stores to get your materials. I have found great craft supplies and wreath embellishments in these types of stores, and it is definitely helpful for the budget.

Basic Supplies

Fabric Protector: A light spray will protect your projects from stains, especially those wreaths with artificial flowers. Use the spray on outdoor wreaths to protect them from the elements, but also on indoor wreaths, especially if they will be displayed in high-traffic locations or where food is being prepared or eaten.

Fabric Scissors: These are great for cutting ribbons or for embellishments such as felt for flowers and leaves. My favorite brand is Fiskars®, which I have had forever, and proof that if you take care of certain things they will last a long time.

Floral Wire: I use green floral wire to wrap small bunches of flowers to each other and to secure them to a wreath form. Floral wire can be used in place of glue or in addition to a little glue to make sure everything is sturdy and remains in place.

Glue and Glue Gun: I use regular clear glue sticks for general crafting. I recommend that you buy these in bulk whenever you can find them on sale because you use a lot of glue to secure all of the elements to your wreaths. Since both the glue and the glue gun can get very hot, please use caution.

Paint or Stain: When you can't find exactly what you are looking for in the store, don't be afraid to do a little extra yourself by painting or staining a plain base or form with your favorite color, especially when the end result will be exactly what you want!

My favorite paint is chalk paint, and chalk paints now come as spray paints. I love chalk paints because whatever you are painting requires almost no prepping.

A light coat of clear matte or gloss spray paint will further protect your wreaths after painting or staining them.

Pipe Cleaners: Though they come in an assortment of colors, I try to match the pipe cleaners with the main color of the wreath; for example, I used tan pipe cleaners for my burlap wreath project.

Tie Wraps: These come in various lengths and colors. I prefer clear tie wraps for wreath making. Use these to secure the elements of the wreath to each other or to the form. I also use tie wraps to create many of my bows so that they will not unravel. Don't worry about the length of the wraps because once they are "closed," you can trim off the excess. I always add a small drop of glue to each of the tie wraps after they are trimmed.

Wire Cutters: You don't need to spend a lot of money on these, but they should fit into your hand comfortably and have good grips. Use these to cut and clean up stray twigs from grapevine wreaths and to trim artificial flowers. I have them in various sizes, but you can do what you need with a basic size.

Project Supplies

Wreath Forms come in an assortment of materials, shapes, and sizes. My favorites are wire wreath forms, embroidery hoops, and grapevine wreaths, but you can also use extruded foam, forms made out of hay or twigs, pool noodles, or even an expanded wire hanger. Wreaths are usually round, but that doesn't have to be the case! You can make a square or oval picture frame, a chalkboard, a garden hose, or even an old wagon or bicycle wheel into a beautiful door or wall hanging.

Burlap comes in an assortment of colors, textures, and price points. Some burlap has finished edges and some is left raw.

Artificial Flowers, Leaves, and Fruits come in all shapes and sizes. Generally speaking, you get what you pay for, so when it comes to artificial elements try to find ones that look as real as possible; however, if that is not available to you at your store or within your budget, just keep in mind that you can improve the look of your wreath by the way you arrange the elements or by adding a lot of texture. If you're unsure of which flowers look good together, look for mini-bouquets because someone has already chosen flower combinations for you. Again, don't rule out the dollar store or thrift store.

If you find that your flowers need a little refreshing either before you use them or once they are already part of your wreath, simply brush them lightly with a microfiber duster. If the flowers are very dusty, put a cup of loose table salt into a small bag, add each flower to the bag, seal the bag, and shake gently to help remove the dust.

Embellishments are the extras you will use on your wreath. Unless you are a total minimalist, you are going to want to adorn your wreath in a special way. This will help you to express your theme creatively. I call everything other than artificial flowers and ribbons embellishments. You can also add interest and another layer to your project with the use of chipboard or metal words, letters, or signs.

Ribbon is sometimes all you need to tie everything together. There are so many beautiful ribbon colors, patterns, and textures. I prefer wired ribbon that is roughly 1 to 2½ inches wide. My ribbon collection is ever-growing, and as you'll soon see from my projects, I am totally obsessed with plaid and gingham ribbon!

You can use good sharp scissors to cut wired ribbon, just be careful if you expose any of the wire thread since it is very sharp. If the wire does extend, simply fold it over to hide it behind the ribbon fabric.

Twine is discreet but also sturdy enough to use for hanging a wreath. Use twine to attach a loop to the back of the wreath so you can hang it on a wreath hook.

Winter

WINTER is the perfect time to embrace all things crafty. When the temperature is cold outside, you can stay warm indoors in your most comfy clothing and work on your seasonal and holiday decor. Let's not forget all the homemade gifts you can create too! Inspiration is everywhere this time of year. Stores will be bombarding your senses with sights, sounds, and scents of the season, so don't be afraid to draw inspiration from these holiday settings to sketch out some ideas or to snap a picture to put in your inspiration folder.

When I think of a perfect craft for winter, the first thing that comes to mind is a beautiful winter wreath for my front door with a combination of fabric leaves, flowers, holly berries, and other wintry decorations. Attach a rich velvet or plaid ribbon, and I'm totally in my element. Are you ready to get started crafting? Grab a cup of your favorite cocoa and let's get creative making a winter wreath!

Embroidery Hoop Wreath

I love this wreath because it is simple, yet elegant and pretty. The best thing is that the idea for it started when I found a few embroidery hoops around the house that I was unlikely to use for embroidery. I immediately started thinking of how I could repurpose them. An embroidery hoop makes an elegant frame for a wintry mix of fabric leaves and flowers, bleached pinecones, berries, velvet ribbons, or anything else you'd like to add.

BASIC SUPPLIES

- Low-grit sandpaper
- Glue gun
- Glue sticks
- Ribbon or cord for hanging
- Wire cutters

VARIATIONS

1. Insert a lace fabric into the embroidery hoop for an elegant touch, or change the style of the project by using a plaid or patterned fabric inside the embroidery hoop and embellishing the outside with flowers and items that coordinate with the fabric.

2. To add more impact to your decor, make several hoop wreaths of different sizes, decorated similarly, and display them side by side or in a pattern.

PROJECT SUPPLIES

- 12-inch wood embroidery hoop
- Paint or stain of your choice
- Clear matte sealant
- Fabric flowers, such as ivory roses
- 2 bunches of green fabric leaves, such as fuzzy elephant ears
- 2 stems of white berries
- 2 bunches of ficus leaves
- 5 pinecones
- 2 pieces of decorative velvet ribbon, ⅞ inch wide by 22 inches long (for loop) and ⅞ inch wide by 32 inches long (for bow)

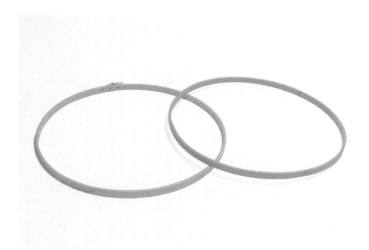

Figure 1

Figure 4

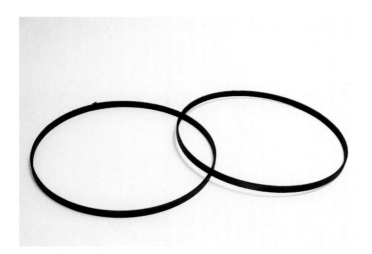

Figure 2

Figure 3

Separate the embroidery hoop into two parts and lightly sand each part of the hoop to make sure there are no rough edges. *Figure 1*

Paint or stain both parts of your hoop following manufacturer's instructions for use, ventilation, and drying time. *Figure 2*

After the paint or stain is dry on both parts, apply a clear matte sealant on both parts to protect the hoop, especially if the wreath will be used outdoors.

When the sealant is dry, put the two parts of the embroidery hoop back together, and tighten the screw to secure. *Figure 3*

From the stems of white berries, clip off several of the branches for embellishing your wreath. *Figure 4*

Assemble your leaves, pinecones, flowers, and berries around the hoop before gluing to get a feel for how you would like your finished wreath to look. *Figure 5*

Using a generous amount of hot glue, affix your leaves to the frame, followed by the berries, flowers, and pinecones. *Figure 6*

With one piece of decorative ribbon, form a loop around the top portion of the hoop and glue the ends together to make a circle. With the other piece of ribbon, tie a bow around the top portion of the loop so that the ends hang down. Your wreath is now ready for hanging.

Figure 5

Figure 6

Cotton Wreath

The beauty of untouched, freshly fallen snow was my inspiration for this wreath made with cotton and light-colored berry twigs. Cotton, like snow, is soft, fluffy, and white. Being a tactile person, I love the feel and look of varying textures in my projects, and that's what makes this wreath unique. The buffalo-plaid ribbon is a favorite of mine, and the bright red color provides a dramatic contrast against the white cotton.

BASIC SUPPLIES

- Floral wire, pipe cleaners, or tie wraps
- Glue gun
- Glue sticks
- Ribbon or cord for hanging
- Wire cutters

PROJECT SUPPLIES

- 18-inch grapevine wreath form
- Cotton bud stems, with 8–12 branches of cotton buds
- One large branch of artificial gray berry twigs
- Wired decorative ribbon, 2–2½ inches wide by 2 yards long

Make your own decorative bow for this wreath. See Tutorial on page 110.

VARIATIONS

1. Decorate your cotton wreath form with seasonal flowers and berries.

2. Purchase cotton that is already decorated with glitter or crystals to add another dimension to your wreath. If you can't find pre-decorated cotton, make your own by spraying the plain cotton with some glitter spray. For added texture, use a little bit of spray adhesive and then sprinkle with small- or medium-sized glitter icicle crystals in clear or silver.

Figure 1

Figure 4

Figure 2

Before getting started, decide which part of the wreath will look best as the top. Since these wreaths are often made by hand, they are sometimes not completely circular. *Figure 1*

Prepare your grapevine wreath by gently cutting off dried leaves and loose vines. *Figure 2*

Select several branches of cotton buds to decorate your wreath. *Figure 3*

Following the shape of your wreath, insert the branches of the cotton buds around the wreath. *Figure 4*

Secure the cotton to the grapevine wreath using glue, floral wire, pipe cleaners, or tie wraps. Layer in additional cotton buds on top of the cotton already in place.

Clip off several branches of gray berries from the twigs to embellish the cotton buds after they have been placed. *Figures 5 & 6*

Affix a decorative bow; select a color that will contrast well with the cotton. *Figure 7*

Attach ribbon or cord behind the wreath for hanging.

Figure 3

Figure 5

Figure 6

Figure 7

Vintage Ornament Wreath

As a little girl at Christmastime, I loved when my mom would open that "special" ornament box to decorate our tree. While she carefully cradled every ornament that came out of this container, she would tell me each one's special story of where it came from and to whom it belonged. Now, I have the same tradition with my own daughter, and it's the perfect time to reminisce and pass along our family stories to her. I wanted this wreath to be fun and kitschy. You can personalize your wreath to match your own holiday colors and style.

BASIC SUPPLIES

- Floral wire (optional)
- Glue gun
- Glue sticks

VARIATIONS

1. Use only gold or only silver ornaments for a simple yet elegant wreath.

2. Make a Halloween wreath! After gluing your ornaments to the form, spray paint the entire wreath black. Add googly eyes, little legs, and faux spider webbing to a few of the ornaments to make spooky spiders on your wreath.

PROJECT SUPPLIES

- 18-inch artificial gold pine wreath base
- 14 large ornaments
- 40 medium ornaments
- 35 small ornaments
- 2 unique-shaped ornaments
- Burlap or thick cord for hanging
- Heavy-duty hook

Figure 1

Figure 2

Figure 4

Figure 3

Assemble a unique assortment of ornaments by size. This wreath was made with a combination of plastic unbreakable ornaments and glass ornaments, some vintage and some from a local craft store. If you prefer to use ornaments that are special to your family, do not glue them on permanently but instead use floral wire to attach them to the base. Either way, make sure the little cap end is secure on each of the ornaments.

Starting with the largest ornaments, affix these around the center of the wreath in a circle. *Figures 1 & 2*

Next, secure the medium-sized ornaments to the wreath on the inside and outside of the circle you just formed with the large ornaments. *Figures 3 & 4*

When placing the ornaments, keep them as close as possible to each other for the best finished look. Add glue to the sides of each ornament in addition to the bottom if needed.

Affix the two unique-shaped ornaments in the lower right-hand corner to add a pop of diversity and interest. Finials or a shape slightly different from the other ornaments will work well.

Use the smallest ornaments to fill in any gaps or spaces you see between the ornaments already secured to the wreath. *Figure 5*

Since this wreath is fragile and likely heavier than an average wreath, hang on a heavy-duty hook with a thick burlap cord, doubled if necessary, to form the loop for hanging.

Figure 5

Evergreen Holiday Wreath

My grandmother always loved red cardinals, so these birds hold a special place in our family. Some people believe that a cardinal is a symbol of a loved one who has passed and when you get a visit from a cardinal, your loved one is with you. Whether you believe this or not, the cardinal is such a beautiful bird and makes a nice addition to this Christmas arrangement. I crafted this wreath to always keep Gram close to our hearts during the holidays.

BASIC SUPPLIES

- Floral wire, pipe cleaners, or tie wraps
- Glue gun
- Glue sticks
- Ribbon or cord for hanging
- Wire cutters

VARIATIONS

1. Embellish with a small plaque that says "Merry" or a similar holiday greeting.

2. Add in small, glittery snowflakes among the greenery.

PROJECT SUPPLIES

- 18-inch grapevine wreath form
- Fabric evergreen branches with or without glitter
- Seasonal fabric flowers such as a bouquet of wintry white flowers
- Decorative elements, such as sprigs of red berries, glittery sprigs, and artificial red cardinals
- 4 pinecones
- Wired decorative ribbon, 2–2½ inches wide by 10 feet long

Make your own decorative bow for this wreath. See Tutorial on page 110.

Figure 1

Figure 2

Figure 3

Figure 4

Decide what the top of your wreath will be. Prepare your wreath by gently cutting off loose vines or dried leaves. *Figure 1*

Trim your evergreen branches so they can be inserted into the spaces of the grapevine wreath. *Figure 2*

Place the evergreens in a pleasing arrangement on one side of the wreath. Directly opposite this position, arrange another grouping of evergreen branches. When you're happy with the effect, glue them to secure in place. Attach more evergreens to fill out the wreath, and add 2 pinecones to each side. *Figures 3 & 4*

Use floral wire or tie wraps in various spots around the wreath to secure your work. *Figure 5*

Separate the flowers from the bouquet. *Figure 6*

After you decide how you will arrange the flowers, you can add them directly to the wreath form or secure the flowers together with floral wire and glue to create a swag. *Figure 7*

Embellish your winter wreath with decorative elements such as a few sprigs of red berries, glittery sprigs, or even a couple of Northern cardinals! *Figures 8 & 9*

Attach ribbon or cord behind the wreath for hanging.

Figure 5

Figure 6

Figure 7

Figure 8

Figure 9

Snowman Wreath

I love the first snowfall of winter, perhaps that's why I'm partial to snowmen. In fact, I have quite a collection of rustic snowmen at home. Here's a snowman wreath that I enjoyed making with my daughter. It's perfect to do with your own junior crafter! When the Christmas wreath gets put away, the snowman wreath replaces it and reminds us that the winter months are still filled with fun. My daughter loves to hear the jingle bells ring every time the front door is opened.

BASIC SUPPLIES

- Clear tie wraps
- Glue gun
- Glue sticks
- Ribbon or cord for hanging
- Scissors
- Wire cutters (with supervision)

VARIATIONS

1. To make the project look more festive, add a small flower, red berries, or a snowflake to the snowman's hat, scarf, or body.

2. Replace the white fairy lights with colored twinkling lights for a different look.

PROJECT SUPPLIES

- 8-inch grapevine wreath form for the head
- 18-inch grapevine wreath form for the body
- White chalk spray paint
- Decorative ribbon, child's scarf, or fabric scrap for scarf
- 2 popsicle sticks
- Small black plastic top hat
- 6 jingle bells
- Red ribbon 1½ inches wide that is long enough to fit band on top hat
- Red ribbon 1½ inches wide by 36 inches long
- 2 or 3 six-foot-long strands of fairy lights
- Seasonal decorations such as 1 or 2 small pinecones and short evergreen branches

Figure 1

Figure 4

Figure 2

Figure 3

Prepare your grapevine wreaths by gently cutting off loose vines or dried leaves. Spray paint both wreaths following manufacturer's instructions for use, ventilation, and drying time.

After the paint is dry on both wreaths, use clear tie wraps to attach the smaller wreath at the top of the larger wreath to form the snowman's head and body. *Figures 1 & 2*

Tie a decorative ribbon, child's scarf, or fabric scrap around the neck area for the snowman's scarf. Arrange it so that it will cover the tie wraps used to connect the wreaths. *Figure 3*

Cut the top hat in half. Glue red ribbon above the brim to form a band. Embellish the hat with the evergreen branches and 1 or 2 small pinecones. *Figure 4*

Insert 2 popsicle sticks about 2 inches apart at the top of the smaller wreath, slightly off center on the right side, and glue to secure. Cover the popsicle sticks with the top hat, making sure that the popsicle sticks are completely hidden by the hat before the glue is applied. *Figures 5 & 6*

Wrap two or three lengths of cool white fairy lights around the body of the snowman. *Figure 7*

Double the red ribbon to make a strip down the center of the snowman's body. Mark off about 4 inches from each end of the folded ribbon and glue your first jingle bell starting at the top. Space your jingle bells an equal distance apart from each other. Glue to the back of the large circle so jingle bells will face out. *Figure 8*

Attach ribbon or cord behind the wreath for hanging.

Figure 5

Figure 7

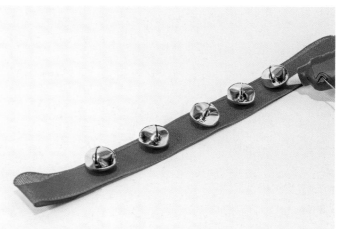

Figure 6

Figure 8

Winter Eucalyptus Wreath

A wreath made with different shades of the same color is stunning. This wreath of winter greens was inspired by my trip to Ireland. As we were descending into Shannon Airport, my view out the window that morning was dazzling—there were so many different shades of green grass that I'll never forget that sight! While this wreath doesn't have as many hues as Ireland's grass, I believe it's a good start!

BASIC SUPPLIES

- Floral wire or clear tie wraps
- Glue gun
- Glue sticks
- Ribbon or cord for hanging
- Wire cutters

PROJECT SUPPLIES

- 28-inch sunburst grapevine wreath form
- 5 or 6 bundles of silver dollar eucalyptus
- 2 bundles of winter greens, separated
- Seasonal decorations such as weathered metal stars

VARIATIONS

1. To bring in another color besides the greens, insert small white berries around the wreath and add a white ribbon.

2. Spray a thin layer of spray glitter to look like a snowy, winter day.

Figure 1

Figure 4

Figure 2

Figure 3

Prepare your grapevine wreath by pulling off any dried leaves. Lie your wreath flat for decorating. *Figure 1*

Separate your bundles of green leaves. Use your wire cutters to cut off branches and separate them into piles. *Figures 2 & 3*

Following the shape of the wreath, glue branches around the wreath a little bit at a time. *Figures 4 & 5*

Continue to glue on the branches until the wreath is covered fully with greens. *Figure 6*

Use glue or floral wire to affix the branches of silver dollar eucalyptus around the wreath. *Figure 7*

Add decorative elements evenly spaced on the wreath.

Attach ribbon or cord behind the wreath for hanging.

Figure 5

Figure 6

Figure 7

Spring

SUNSHINE in spring really makes me smile, especially after a cold and gloomy winter. Birds, flowers, and trees are bursting with life. In springtime, I love being outdoors, working in the garden, and planting vegetables and herbs. The good weather always puts me in the mood to create something new. In spring, I absorb all the positive energy of the season—butterflies, birds, flowers, and even spring showers to inspire my selection of wreaths and door hangings.

Upcycling and recycling are very important to me. For instance, instead of throwing away an old garden hose I had from last season, I decided to turn it into a unique wreath. Adding ivy, raspberries, and a brightly colored spring ribbon to tie everything together, I now have an inviting decoration for my front door. On a perfect day, I like to move all my crafting supplies to the wooden picnic table in the backyard and craft with my daughter. We make a pitcher of iced tea, put on some music, and get crafty!

Wire Hoop Wreath

The softness of felt flowers paired with the texture of the chicken wire is what makes this wreath so eye-catching! I like using chicken wire as a base because it lies flatter than most wreaths; it's perfect if you don't have much space between your entrance and screen doors. Though the design is basic, you can elevate it with the decorations you select. I like to make my own felt flowers because you get to be as creative as you want. You can choose your own color schemes or even make up completely new types of flowers!

BASIC SUPPLIES

- Glue gun

- Glue sticks

- Soft cloth

- Sturdy gloves or cut-resistant gloves (optional)

- Wire cutters

VARIATIONS

1. Experiment with flowers in different colors for different seasons. You can never have too many flowers! Add enough flowers to cover half of the wreath form.

2. If you don't want to work with chicken wire, substitute a 10-inch wooden embroidery hoop for the metal wire hoop. Instead of chicken wire, select a sheer lace fabric to fill the hoop and then place the felt flowers.

PROJECT SUPPLIES

- 10-inch metal wire hoop form

- 12-inch square of galvanized chicken wire (sold in craft stores in 12-inch by 50-inch rolls)

- 8 felt flowers

- 8–10 green felt leaves

- 9-inch by 12-inch piece of green felt for base

- 2 ⅜-inch by 10-yard rolls of decorative ribbon in different colors to match felt flowers

Make your own felt flowers and leaves for this wreath.
See Tutorials on pages 106-108.

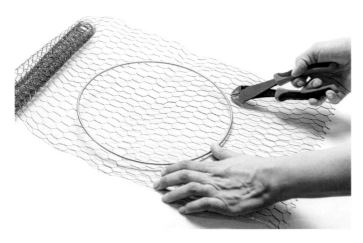

Figure 1

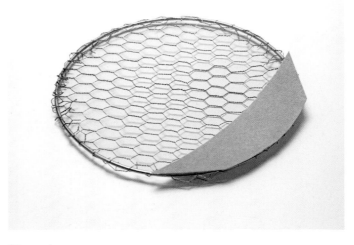

Figure 4

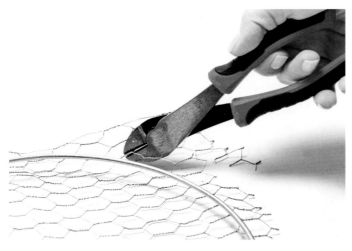

Figure 2

Wipe down the metal hoop form with a soft cloth so it's clean, and place the hoop form over a section of chicken wire.

Carefully cut the chicken wire by following a one-cell perimeter around the outside of the hoop. *Figures 1 & 2*

Secure the chicken wire to the metal hoop form by folding over the ends of the chicken wire so they are securely wrapped around the rim. Wearing protective gloves is recommended. *Figure 3*

Cut a semicircle arc from the green felt to make a base for the flowers and leaves. You will glue it to the bottom part of the hoop when your flower arrangement is complete. *Figure 4*

Decide how you want to arrange the flowers and leaves and then glue them to the felt piece. *Figures 5 & 6*

Affix the decorated felt base to the chicken wire.

Secure one piece of decorative ribbon to the hoop form and glue the end. Weave the ribbon in and out through the outermost cells of the chicken wire (this project shows white ribbon as the base color). When the rim is covered in your base color, go in and out of every other cell with your second color. *Figures 7 & 8*

With a piece of ribbon about 26 inches long, pass the ribbon through a space at the top of the rim, basically folding the ribbon in half, and leaving a loop of about 4 inches before tying a knot. Make a bow over the knot to finish off. Your wreath is now ready for hanging.

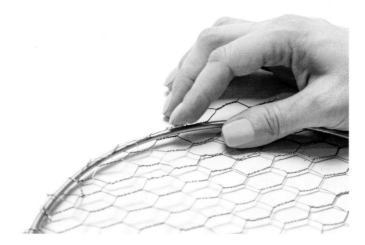

Figure 3

Figure 5

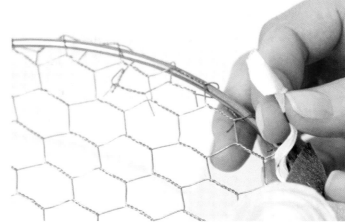

Figure 7

Figure 6

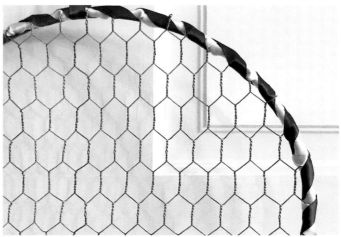

Figure 8

Garden Hose Wreath

"Everything old is new again!" My husband has stopped asking me "Why are we saving this?" He has now resigned himself to the fact that many times he will see something stored in my house or garage that will later show up in another place—but completely upcycled! I am happy that we are all trying to do our part to help the environment. While this garden hose could have been discarded last season, it's making me happy that it is looking so elegant in its new setting.

BASIC SUPPLIES

- Clear tie wraps
- Glue gun
- Glue sticks
- Ribbon or cord for hanging
- Wire cutters

PROJECT SUPPLIES

- Garden hose, about 25 feet needed
- Fabric flowers
- Fabric leaves in a vine, such as ivy
- 2 bunches of red berries
- Wired decorative ribbon, 2–2½ inches wide by 8 feet long

VARIATIONS

1. Embellish hose wreath with seed packets.

2. Affix a small gardening shovel and colorful gardening gloves to the wreath.

Make your own decorative bow for this wreath. See Tutorial on page 110.

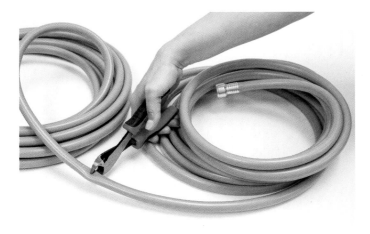

Figure 1

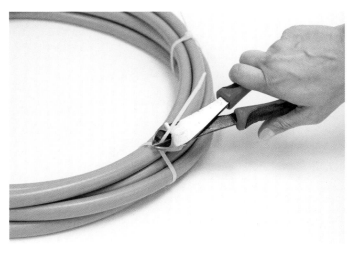

Figure 4

Figure 2

Cut garden hose, if needed, to make it about 25 feet long. Roll garden hose into a loose circle to form the wreath base. *Figures 1 & 2*

Using clear tie wraps, secure the hose tightly in 4 or 5 places to help wreath keep its shape, and cut off the long ends. Add a drop of glue to each tie wrap to keep it in place. *Figures 3 & 4*

Gather the fabric flowers, leaves, and berries and cut the branches so they will have the best fit around the hose. *Figures 5 & 6*

Place several vines of leaves around the tie wraps, bending and shaping the leaves so the tie wraps are not visible. *Figure 7*

Flowers should be layered on top of the leaves, following the shape of the wreath and covering more than half of the wreath. *Figure 8*

Cut the longer stems off the bunches of berries and add onto the wreath in clusters. *Figure 9*

Embellish with a decorative ribbon on the front, and attach a ribbon or cord behind the wreath for hanging. *Figure 10*

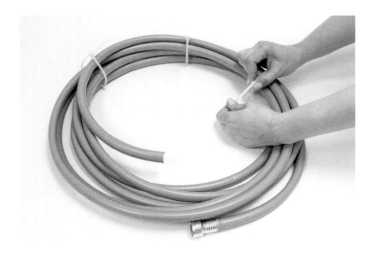

Figure 3

Figure 5

Figure 8

Figure 6

Figure 9

Figure 7

Figure 10

Recycled Paper Wreath

We had a few instructional piano books at home from when my daughter first started her piano lessons. Since many of the pages were dog-eared from use, this wreath was a perfect opportunity to recycle the paper. The music sheets add a personal touch and are not distracting from the wreath itself. The soft and casual denim material used to make the flowers gives a comfortable, homey feel to it, so it's perfect for a den or family room. This wreath would also make a thoughtful gift for a favorite music teacher!

BASIC SUPPLIES

- Glue gun
- Glue sticks
- Pencil, unsharpened
- Ribbon or cord for hanging
- Ruler
- Scissors

PROJECT SUPPLIES

- 16-inch circular wooden wreath form
- White or cream craft paint and foam brush
- Sheet music book or other book for recycling
- Small inkpad, either black or brown
- 8 denim roses

VARIATIONS

1. Replace the handmade denim flowers with store-bought or repurposed artificial flowers.

2. Use a colorful or patterned scrapbook paper instead of the music paper or decorate using a metallic or bright-colored ink.

Make your own denim roses
for this wreath.
See Tutorial on page 104.

Figure 1

Figure 4

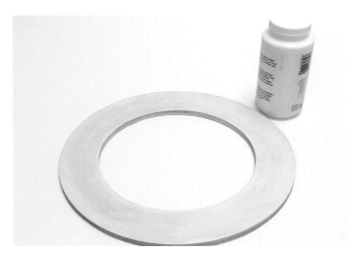

Figure 2

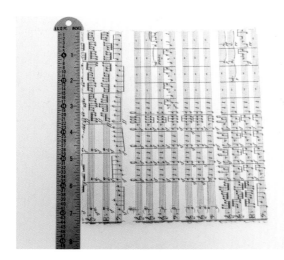

Figure 3

Start with a wooden wreath form and paint it white or cream. *Figure 1*

Remove the pages from your book. Trim them down to roughly 7-inch squares. Any size will work as long as it is square. Using smaller square sheets will make the wreath shorter and flatter, while making the squares larger will add depth and height. *Figures 2 & 3*

Distress the pages by brushing all four edges along the top of an inkpad. *Figure 4*

Using an unsharpened pencil, place the pencil in the center of each sheet and fold it quickly by wrapping the paper around the pencil. *Figure 5*

Add a drop of hot glue at the folded center of the paper so that it adheres to the wreath form. Start the first paper near the inner part of the ring; continue adding papers until the whole circle is fully covered. *Figure 6*

Add denim roses in a cluster slightly off center at the bottom of the wreath. *Figure 7*

Attach ribbon or cord behind the wreath for hanging.

Figure 5

Figure 6

Figure 7

Umbrella Door Hanging

"April showers bring May flowers." Speaking of showers, this is a perfect project to do with your young crafter on a rainy day. Though you can use any type of fabric flower, I chose Gerbera daisies for this project because they come in a variety of bold, bright colors, and you're sure to find colors that match the umbrella selected for the flower holder. Plus, since your umbrella already has a hook handle, as soon as it's finished it will be ready to display!

BASIC SUPPLIES

- Floral wire, pipe cleaners, or tie wraps
- Glue gun
- Glue sticks
- Wire cutters (with supervision)

PROJECT SUPPLIES

- Child-sized umbrella with a hook handle
- Fabric flowers, such as Gerbera daisies, enough to make a small bouquet shape
- Fabric leaves
- One floral foam block, approximately 3 inches x 4 inches x 8 inches, or fabric scraps
- Wired decorative ribbon, 2–2½ inches wide by 3 feet long
- Strong fishing line (optional)

VARIATIONS

1. Hang the umbrella at an angle by attaching clear fishing line from the base of the umbrella to the handle. Then hang your umbrella on a wreath hook.

2. Decorating for a baby shower? Start with a white umbrella and fill it with pink, blue, or yellow flowers, or a combination of all three colors.

Figure 1

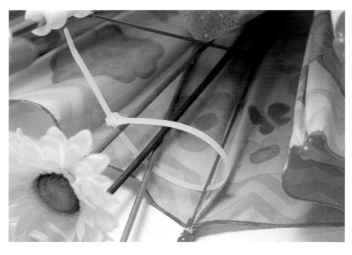

Figure 4

Figure 2

Select a child-sized umbrella in crafter's choice of design. Insert a floral foam block inside the umbrella under the spokes to keep the body slightly open to allow for decoration. If you don't have a foam block, several pieces of scrap fabric will work as well. *Figure 1*

Try the flowers in the umbrella to decide if any will need to be cut. Trim the longer stems with wire cutters. Insert additional floral foam or fabric scraps into the umbrella if your flower stems need more length. *Figures 2 & 3*

Attach the flowers to each other and to the umbrella spokes with a combination of tie wraps and glue. Don't forget to cut off the long ends of the tie wraps. *Figures 4 & 5*

Insert the flowers into the umbrella opening so they are slightly overhanging the edge. *Figure 6*

Trim the fabric leaves to the desired length and insert them into the opening the same way as the flowers. *Figure 7*

Wrap decorative ribbon around the middle of the umbrella. *Figure 8*

Use the umbrella handle to hang the wreath.

Figure 3

Figure 5

Figure 7

Figure 6

Figure 8

Pastel Butterfly Wreath

Another lovely sign of spring, the first sighting of a butterfly reminds me not to take things too seriously and to enjoy the little moments. A dear friend of mine actually calls these light, feathery, flying insects "flutterbies," which apparently is not so uncommon—it's a child-like way to say butterflies. Though real butterflies come in a variety of bright colors, the pastel fabric butterflies enhance the spring greenery in this delicate wreath.

BASIC SUPPLIES

- Floral wire, pipe cleaners, or tie wraps
- Glue gun
- Glue sticks
- Wire cutters

PROJECT SUPPLIES

- 14-inch wire wreath form
- 2 six-foot-long garlands of spring greenery, such as boxwood
- 2 bunches of varied spring greenery
- 12 fabric butterflies in pastel shades
- 12 small pink flowers
- Wired decorative ribbon, 1½–2 inches wide by 30 inches long

VARIATIONS

1. Use butterflies that are all the same color and include a small bird for embellishment.

2. Use a boxwood wreath form in place of the wire wreath form.

Figure 1

Figure 2

Figure 3

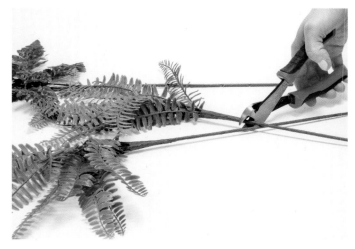

Figure 4

Start the base of the wreath by wrapping the boxwood garlands tightly around the wire wreath form. *Figure 1*

Continue to keep the garland snug as you wrap it around the form until it is completely covered. *Figure 2*

Use wire cutters to separate and cut the extra greenery. *Figure 3*

Use the greenery to decorate the wreath and make it more full. Cut small, wispy ferns to arrange in all directions so that the ferns stick out in various places, which will add texture to the wreath. *Figures 4 & 5*

Trim the flowers and affix them randomly around the wreath. *Figure 6*

Place the butterflies on the wreath; when you're happy with the arrangement, glue each butterfly with a drop of glue to the greenery. *Figure 7*

Pass decorative ribbon through the top opening of the wire in the back of the wreath and double knot a few inches from the ends for hanging.

Figure 5

Figure 6

Figure 7

Tulip-time Wreath

Tulips are one of my favorite types of flowers. The tulips in my garden bloom every spring, and I always feel happy when I see the first signs of them. I love that tulips are so easy to grow and come in such beautiful colors. Many people associate the different colors with certain characteristics. I've chosen white and pink shades for this wreath because the colors are relaxing and soft and harmonize well. Pink tulips are said to symbolize caring and good wishes; white tulips are said to represent purity and respect. For me, tulips of any color are enchanting because I'm a hopeless romantic at heart!

BASIC SUPPLIES

- Floral wire, pipe cleaners, or tie wraps
- Glue gun
- Glue sticks
- Ribbon or cord for hanging
- Wire cutters

PROJECT SUPPLIES

- 18-inch grapevine wreath
- 10–12 tulips in pink and white with leaves (or pick your own colors)
- Two bunches of greenery
- 2 coordinating patterns of wired ribbon, each 1½ inches wide by 3 feet long
- Spray paint in white or gray (optional)

Make your own decorative bow for this wreath.
See Tutorial on page 109.

VARIATIONS

1. Assemble flowers in a group and secure to the side, leaving most of the wreath exposed. Place a bow below the flowers.

2. Use three colors of tulips and arrange in the same direction to follow the shape of the wreath so that the whole wreath form is covered in tulips and looks very full.

Figure 1

Figure 4

Figure 2

Prepare your grapevine wreath by gently cutting off loose vines or dried leaves.

Leave your wreath its natural color or spray paint the wreath in white, gray, or color of your choice. If spray painting, follow the manufacturer's instructions for use, ventilation, and drying. *Figure 1*

Start with a base of greenery on one side of your wreath. Trim the stems so they will follow the shape of the wreath. Use the spaces on the grapevine wreath to weave in the tips before gluing to secure. *Figures 2 & 3*

Affix a similar arrangement on the opposite side of the wreath. *Figure 4*

Visualize how you want to arrange your tulips and leaves on the wreath to get a feel for your finished project. *Figure 5*

Trim off any longer stems and leaves that would protrude from the wreath. *Figure 6*

Using the long tulip leaves for the base of the wreath, intertwine the ends in the larger spaces of the grapevine wreath. *Figures 7 & 8*

Make 2 simple bows in coordinating patterns following the tutorial on page 109. For this project, cut the tails at 45-degree angles and keep the tails short so that they are not much longer than the loops of the bows. After you have secured the tie wraps at the center of each of the bows, turn one bow upside down on top of the other so that its tails are facing up. Cut a 6-inch strip from one of the remaining ribbon pieces and wrap it around the centers of both bows and tie a simple knot.

Figure 3

Attach ribbon or cord behind the wreath for hanging.

Figure 5

Figure 7

Figure 6

Figure 8

Summer

SUMMER days remind me it's time to slow down a little and relax by doing things I love, such as going to the beach and spending time with friends. Since the days are longer, I feel like I have more time to squeeze in some fun . . . and maybe even get to finish reading a book as I soak up some sun! Because I love the beach so much, my favorite theme for summer crafting and decorating is nautical. I have to admit that unless I have my house decorated for a special holiday, I enjoy this look in my home year-round. You can use shells, rope, and moss in your crafts to bring the beach indoors.

Summertime is also the season for graduations, Father's Day, Fourth of July and Labor Day barbecues, and don't forget birthdays and showers. There are many opportunities to create unique crafts for these special occasions. Go pour yourself a tall glass of lemonade, and let's get crafting!

Picture Frame Door or Wall Hanging

I purchased this oval picture frame at my local craft store, but you can easily repurpose an old frame of any shape or size. My daughter selected the lime-colored gingham ribbon and brightly colored flowers to match the color scheme in her bedroom. I love that she is enjoying making crafts to decorate her space with her own style and preferences. This picture frame hanging would also be a great homemade gift for a young crafter to personalize for a grandmother or special aunt.

BASIC SUPPLIES

- Glue gun
- Glue sticks
- Wire cutters (with supervision)

PROJECT SUPPLIES

- White oval picture frame, any size
- Fabric flowers such as ranunculus
- One bunch of fabric leaves such as ferns
- 2 pieces of wired decorative ribbon, 1–2 inches wide by 10 inches long and 1–2 inches wide by 18 inches long

VARIATIONS

1. Cut a corkboard the shape of the frame and cover it with fabric. Glue the fabric down on the back of the board. Outline the inner border of the frame with glue, then press the frame against the fabric side of the corkboard until it holds. You now have a pretty hanging corkboard!

2. Make a bedroom mirror! Find a mirror the same size as the frame or have one cut to fit the size of the frame. Outline the inner border of the frame with glue, then press the front of the mirror on the glue until it holds.

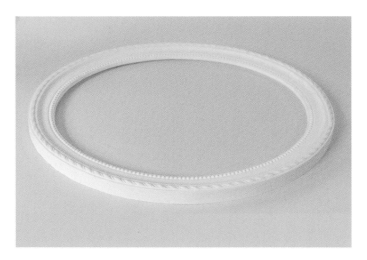

Figure 1

Figure 4

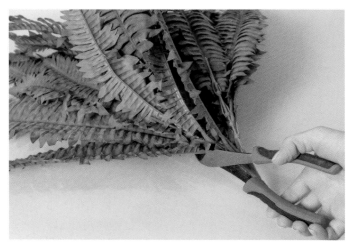

Figure 2

If you're repurposing an old frame, make sure it is dust-free and clean. *Figure 1*

Cut ferns from the bunch in assorted lengths. *Figure 2*

Assemble leaves around the bottom portion of the frame to serve as a base for the flowers. Layer some of the top branches at an angle away from the frame. *Figures 3 & 4*

Trim flowers if needed. Decide how you are going to arrange the flowers before gluing them to the frame. *Figure 5*

Glue flowers to the picture frame. Do a similar arrangement on each side for a balanced look. *Figure 6*

With the shorter piece of decorative ribbon, form a loop around the top portion of the hoop and glue the ends together to make a circle. With the other piece of ribbon, tie a bow around the bottom portion of the loop so that the ends hang down. Your wreath is now ready for hanging. *Figures 7 & 8*

Figure 3

Figure 5

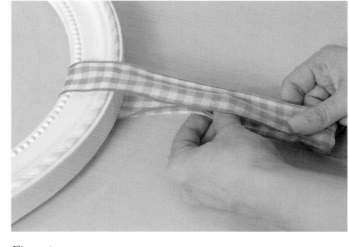

Figure 7

Figure 6

Figure 8

Fourth of July Rag Wreath

This wreath is almost as spectacular as a fireworks display on the Fourth of July! And, it can literally be made from rags if you don't want to spend money on new fabric. So not only is it a good use of repurposing, it's economical as well. But don't let the fact that it's a low-cost project fool you because the finished wreath will surely have a big impact. When some friends saw this wreath at our recent summer barbecue, they couldn't believe I had made it myself—let's just say, it made a BIG BANG!

BASIC SUPPLIES

- Fabric scissors
- Ruler

VARIATIONS

1. Alternate different colors or patterns to customize this wreath for another holiday. Use fall colors to make a Thanksgiving wreath, or orange, black, and white to make a Halloween wreath.

2. Look for a heart-shaped form to make a Valentine's Day wreath or to decorate for a wedding, shower, or anniversary party.

PROJECT SUPPLIES

- 14¼-inch wire wreath form
- One yard each of three different fabrics in red, white, and blue solid colors or patterns
- Store-bought Fourth of July decorations, such as rockets, stars, tinsel sparklers, and glitter curls
- Ribbon or a piece of the leftover fabric for hanging the wreath

Make your own rockets
for this wreath.
See Tutorial on page 112.

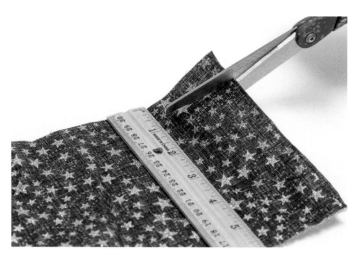

Figure 1

Figure 4

Figure 2

Cut off the selvage (sewn border edges) of the fabrics, if applicable.

Cut and tear all your fabric into strips. You'll need a total of about 200 strips measuring 1 inch wide by 8 inches long. A quick and easy way to do this is to use your ruler and scissors to mark off each inch by making a small cut on the fabric that is already cut to the 8-inch length. Then the fabric should tear easily from the cut mark made with the scissors. *Figure 1*

If the excess frayed edges bother you, simply pull them off or trim them with your fabric scissors.

Separate your fabric into piles based on your colors. *Figure 2*

Fold your fabric in half and slip the free ends under the inner wire on the form. *Figure 3*

Slip the free ends through the loop of the fabric and pull tightly to make a knot. *Figures 4 & 5*

Alternate knotting each piece of fabric until your whole wreath is full. *Figure 6*

Accent with embellishments that match the theme of your fabric. *Figure 7*

Affix a ribbon or a piece of the leftover fabric to hang the wreath.

Figure 3

Figure 5

Figure 6

Figure 7

Colorful Clothespin Wreath

Does anyone buy clothespins anymore for the original intent—to hang clothes? I know I'm dating myself, but when I see a bunch of new clothespins all I can think about is the smell of clean, fresh laundry blowing on an outdoor clothesline. Though I can recall this happy reminiscence from my childhood, I have to admit that these days most of my family's fresh-laundered clothes are going in the dryer! I do, however, have a bunch of clothespins and a craft drawer full of washi tape in a variety of bright summer colors, which inspired me to make this cheerful wreath.

BASIC SUPPLIES

- Cotton swabs
- Fabric scissors
- Glue gun
- Glue sticks
- Ribbon or cord for hanging

VARIATIONS

1. Paint the wreath white, black, or the same color as your front door.

2. Use paint, markers, glitter, or a variety of each instead of washi tape on the clothespins.

PROJECT SUPPLIES

- 14¼-inch wire wreath form
- 125–175 small crafts clothespins, about 1¾ inches long
- Washi tape in a variety of bright colors and patterns (about 4 or 5 different designs)
- White spray paint or color to match clothespin colors
- Mod-Podge® matte sealant
- 3 assorted metal flowers

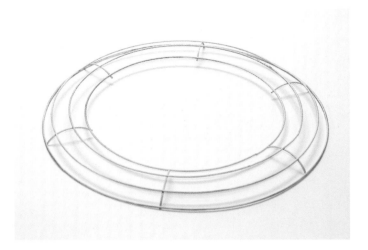

Figure 1

Figure 4

Figure 2

Figure 3

Spray paint a wire wreath according to the manufacturer's instructions. Make sure to give it plenty of time to dry. *Figure 1*

While waiting for the form to dry, start to decorate the clothespins. Stick a strip of the washi tape to one of the long sides of the clothespin. It's okay for it to fold over the side. Cut the end of the strip. Repeat so that you have a minimum of 125 decorated clothespins in four or five different designs. *Figures 2, 3, & 4*

If needed, use a bit of Mod-Podge or glue on the tip of a cotton swab to hold down any loose flaps of washi tape. *Figure 5*

Starting in the innermost ring of the form, attach clothespins following the same pattern all the way around the wreath. Try to keep the clothespins as close to each other as possible on the innermost ring. *Figure 6*

Decide how full or spread out you want the outside portion of your wreath. I've done two rows on this wreath and have left spaces, but you can make your outside portion tight by filling in all the spaces on the middle and outer portions and placing your clothespins tightly together.

Add glue as needed to prevent the clothespins from moving. Seal the entire clothespin wreath with a layer of Mod-Podge.

When your wreath is completely dry, embellish it with small metal flowers by gluing the flowers directly onto the clothespins. *Figure 7*

Attach ribbon or cord behind the wreath for hanging.

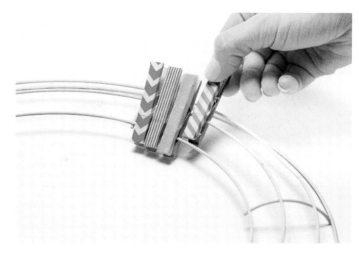

Figure 5

Figure 6

Figure 7

Lemon Blueberry Wreath

When life gives you lemons, make a wreath! A perfect decoration for summer, this wreath mimics one of my favorite summer drinks—blueberry-mint lemonade! Looking at this wreath is as refreshing as the drink (by the way, it's made with lemon juice, water, sugar, blueberries, and mint leaves). I have this sunshiny wreath at the entrance to my mudroom, where it's a cheerful hello to everyone who comes to visit.

BASIC SUPPLIES

- Fabric scissors
- Glue gun
- Glue sticks
- Wire cutters

VARIATIONS

1. Use limes, oranges, or different berries to match a particular color scheme or theme.

2. Substitute white fabric flowers instead of artificial fruit for an entirely different look that would be perfect for a wedding or bridal shower.

PROJECT SUPPLIES

- 18-inch sunburst grapevine wreath form
- 2 large bunches of an assortment of green leaves
- 5–7 artificial lemon branches (each branch usually has 2 lemons)
- 5–6 bunches of artificial blueberries
- 5–6 artificial mint sprigs
- Wired decorative ribbon, 1½–2 inches wide by 30 inches long

Figure 1

Figure 4

Figure 2

Figure 3

Prepare your wreath by gently cutting off loose vines or dried leaves. *Figure 1*

Trim your assortment of green leaves and separate them into different varieties. *Figures 2 & 3*

Start with a base layer of larger stems of similar leaves near the outer edge of the wreath.

Using different leaves of different lengths, place them around the wreath, following the shape of the form. *Figure 4*

When you are happy with the arrangement, glue the greenery to the wreath to secure. Fill in open spaces with additional leaves and branches.

Plan how you will place the lemon arrangements. I always like to use an odd number so I placed 5 branches with 2 lemons on each branch, but you can add more depending on your arrangement. Remove the lemons for now, and place the mint sprigs and the blueberries in those areas; glue to secure. The mint sprigs and blueberries will add variety and texture and will also help the lemons to pop from the greenery for a more dramatic effect. *Figures 5 & 6*

Insert the lemon branches near the blueberries and mint sprigs. *Figure 7*

Wrap decorative ribbon around the top portion of the wreath and tie a knot at the end. Your wreath is now ready for hanging.

Figure 5

Figure 6

Figure 7

Nautical Wreath

Our family recently rented a lakeside house in New Hampshire for a week-long summer vacation. My husband spent many of his summer vacations in the same area when he was growing up, so it was a special treat to be there as a family. I loved having such a restful time, enjoying the fresh air, the fishing, the bike rides, and the sunsets over the lake at night. We had a special time with friends going out on their boat and water surfing, and my daughter has been talking about the fun on the boat since we came home. Though we weren't out on the ocean, this nautical wreath will remind us of our vacation with friends and family.

BASIC SUPPLIES

- Fabric scissors
- Glue gun
- Glue sticks
- Ribbon or cord for hanging
- Wire cutters

PROJECT SUPPLIES

- 18-inch or 24-inch grapevine wreath form
- Gray chalk spray paint (optional)
- Rope netting, like fishing net
- 2 dozen assorted shells (often sold 12 to a bag)
- 3–4 white or cream starfish, one larger than the others
- 1 small bag of moss

VARIATIONS

1. Spray paint your wreath white or blue to create a different nautical look.

2. Keep with the nautical theme by using a small length of nautical rope or twisted colorful cotton rope to hang your wreath.

Figure 1

Figure 4

Figure 2

Figure 3

Prepare your grapevine wreath by gently cutting off loose vines or dried leaves. *Figure 1*

Work with the netting to create a nautical background for the shells and to add some texture to the wreath. If there is excess netting, cut the end with scissors. Glue the netting at the back of the wreath in various places to secure. *Figure 2*

If you want to age the netting a little bit once you have it positioned, use a light coating of gray spray paint to all or parts of the netting. *Figure 3*

Attach moss to the area where the shells will go (almost half of the wreath); this will form a good base and make it easier to glue them. *Figure 4*

Select shells, keeping in mind that you will need a mixture of small, medium, and large shells to cover roughly half of the wreath. *Figure 5*

Select one large starfish to be the focal point. I suggest keeping this one at the center or slightly off-center of the other shells in the arrangement. Arrange the shells and starfish around the wreath so it is visually appealing, then affix the shells to the wreath with glue.

Attach ribbon or cord behind the wreath for hanging.

Figure 5

Succulent and Cork Wreath

Tap your local wine enthusiast for corks to make this unique wreath! If you don't want your wreath wine-stained, you can find bags of corks online or in your local craft store. There are also a variety of faux green succulents available. Succulents are very popular right now. While the process of gluing the corks in a chevron pattern is time-consuming, the finished wreath is beautiful and well worth the time spent on the project. It makes a great gift—and no green thumb required!

BASIC SUPPLIES

- Fabric scissors
- Glue gun
- Glue sticks

PROJECT SUPPLIES

- 15-inch extruded foam wreath form
- 150–200 corks, either new or upcycled
- 10–12 assorted succulents
- 3 feet of decorative wide burlap ribbon for hanging
- Small piece of twine, 6–12 inches long

VARIATIONS

1. Paint corks in all one color or a variety of colors before working on your wreath.

2. Replace faux succulents with real air plants or succulents.

Figure 1

Figure 2

Figure 3

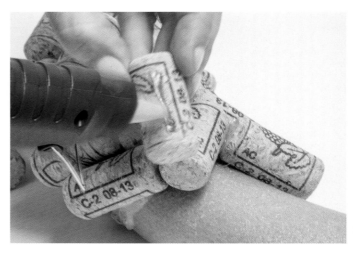

Figure 4

Gather your materials. You will be gluing the corks directly onto the foam form in a chevron pattern. Practice the design before working with the wreath. *Figure 1*

Once you are ready, start by adding glue to either end of the first cork, stick it to the longer side of another cork so the two corks are perpendicular and an upside-down L shape is formed. *Figures 2 and 3*

As you add the corks, glue the side of the cork that will adhere to the wreath as well as continuing to glue one end. *Figure 4*

Once you have started the pattern, continue to add the corks in the same direction so that each piece in the design is following the same angle as the row before it. Continue in this manner to make the chevron pattern. *Figure 5*

Once the wreath is covered with cork, you can affix assorted succulents at the bottom or side of the wreath. *Figures 6 & 7*

Wrap burlap ribbon around the wreath to hang it.

Figure 5

Figure 6

Figure 7

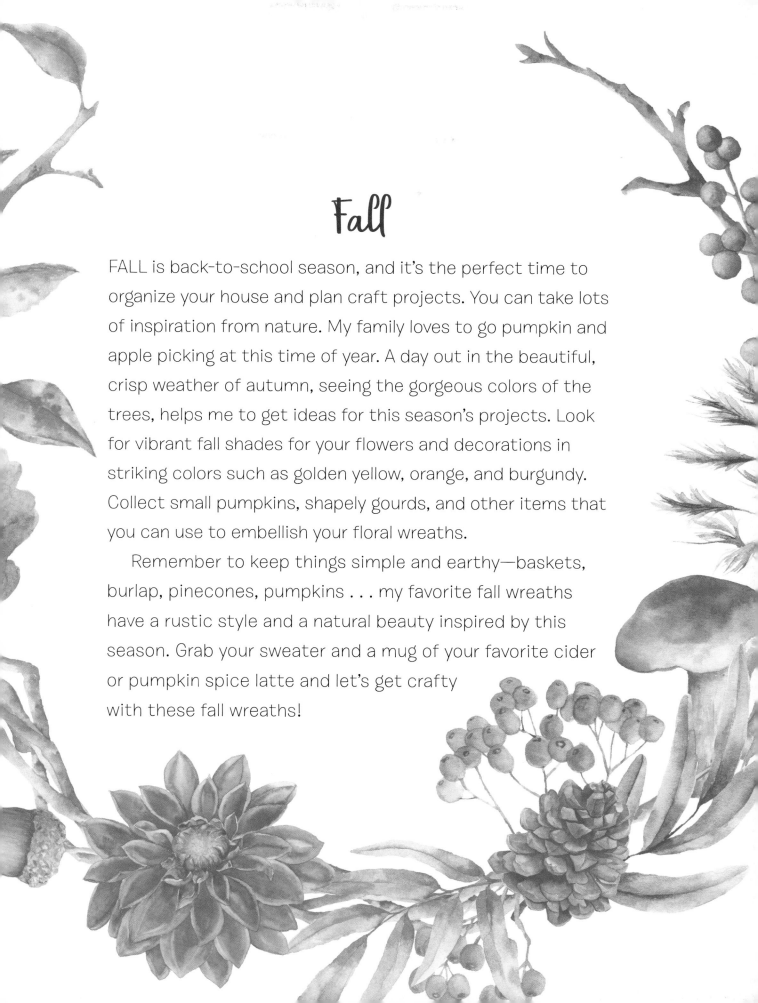

Fall

FALL is back-to-school season, and it's the perfect time to organize your house and plan craft projects. You can take lots of inspiration from nature. My family loves to go pumpkin and apple picking at this time of year. A day out in the beautiful, crisp weather of autumn, seeing the gorgeous colors of the trees, helps me to get ideas for this season's projects. Look for vibrant fall shades for your flowers and decorations in striking colors such as golden yellow, orange, and burgundy. Collect small pumpkins, shapely gourds, and other items that you can use to embellish your floral wreaths.

Remember to keep things simple and earthy—baskets, burlap, pinecones, pumpkins . . . my favorite fall wreaths have a rustic style and a natural beauty inspired by this season. Grab your sweater and a mug of your favorite cider or pumpkin spice latte and let's get crafty with these fall wreaths!

Woven Basket Door Hanging

The flat back of this hanging basket makes it a perfect fit when there isn't a lot of room for a full wreath between the front door and the screen door. It's also a perfect wall hanging for basically anywhere in the house. I love that this project is so simplistic, but when it is finished, it has such a rustic charm and beauty to it. Select a decorative ribbon that appeals to you, and then match a variety of flowers and leaves to complement the colors of the ribbon. Keeping in mind that you will want a flat back, be creative with the shape and style of your basket!

BASIC SUPPLIES

- Glue gun
- Glue sticks
- Wire cutters (with supervision)

PROJECT SUPPLIES

- 14-inch flat-back hanging basket
- Floral foam brick to fit inside your basket
- Seasonal fabric flowers
- Fabric leaves
- Two pieces of wired decorative ribbon, each 2–2½ inches wide by 36 inches long
- Clear matte or glossy spray paint (optional)

VARIATIONS

1. Repurpose this hanging basket for each season by changing the colors of the flowers and the ribbon; try daisies in summer, daffodils in spring, and poinsettias in winter.

2. Decorate several baskets varying either the selection of the ribbons or the selection of the flowers and arrange them in a grouping on the same wall.

Figure 1

Figure 4

Figure 2

Figure 3

Wipe down your basket. If you are going to use this basket outdoors, you will want to coat it with a few coats of clear matte or glossy spray paint. *Figure 1*

Prepare your flowers by trimming off the stems. Make sure the flowers will show above the edge of the basket. Be mindful to vary the heights of the flowers to create visual interest. *Figure 2*

Insert a piece of floral foam to fit into the bottom of the basket. *Figure 3*

Use the floral foam to give the bouquet height or push the flower and leaf stems directly into the foam to hold them in place. *Figure 4*

Arrange the flowers and leaves to fill the basket. Some leaves and flowers should hang over the edge of the basket. *Figure 5*

Place leaves around and within the flowers to fill in spaces and add to the fullness of your bouquet.

After you have the flowers arranged, wrap one piece of decorative ribbon around the outside of the basket, allowing an extra 2 inches to overlap, and glue the ends down. *Figures 6 & 7*

Make a simple bow with the second piece of ribbon and glue it to the front of the basket on top of the ribbon strip. Your basket is now ready to hang! *Figure 8*

Figure 5

Figure 6

Figure 7

Figure 8

Fall Eucalyptus Wreath

Do you know how certain scents can remind you of certain people? Ever since I was a little girl, my mom has always kept a bunch of eucalyptus somewhere in the house. She says the smell of eucalyptus makes it feel like her house is fresh and clean. Even if a bunch of these plants have aged and lost their scent, my mom will start the tea kettle and hold the branches over the steam to clean and refresh them until she is able to pick up a brand-new batch. Because of this, I always like to have eucalyptus in my own house—but in a wreath shape, of course!

BASIC SUPPLIES

- Glue gun
- Glue sticks
- Green floral wire or floral tape
- Ribbon or cord for hanging
- Wire cutters

PROJECT SUPPLIES

- 14-inch wire wreath form
- 2 bunches of eucalyptus, dried or fresh
- 5 assorted 2–4-inch decorative pumpkins and gourds

VARIATIONS

1. Make this eucalyptus wreath and place the decorative pumpkins and gourds in the center of the wreath for a perfect fall table centerpiece.

2. Replace the gourds with dried flowers, herbs, or cotton buds on one side of the wreath; hang with a colorful ribbon.

Figure 1

Figure 4

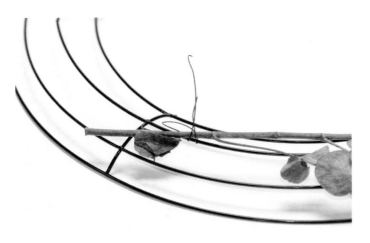

Figure 2

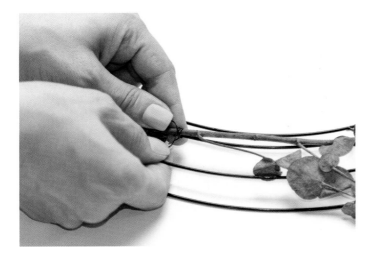

Figure 3

Before starting, lay out your eucalyptus branches around the form to get a feel for how you want your finished wreath to look.

Snip the branches to the correct length to fit the style of the arrangement you have in mind. *Figure 1*

Start the base of the wreath by placing one stem of eucalyptus in the middle of the form. As you work, use floral wire or tape to hold the stems in place. *Figures 2 & 3*

Continue to work around the form with the branches all facing in the same direction, trimming and styling the arrangement as you move around in a circle. *Figures 4 and 5*

Wrap each branch individually until the entire wreath form is covered with branches. *Figure 6*

To fill in blank spaces, make a bundle of small leaves, join the ends together with floral wire or tape, and attach them to the base branches with wire or glue.

Keep in mind that some branches should be pulled out at an angle to give the wreath a wispy appearance. *Figure 7*

On one side of the arrangement, in a tight grouping, glue your decorative pumpkins and gourds to the wreath. *Figure 8*

Attach ribbon or cord behind the wreath for hanging.

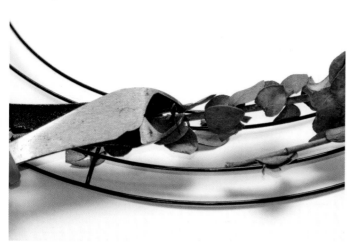

Figure 5

Figure 7

Figure 6

Figure 8

Burlap Farmhouse Wreath

I absolutely love everything about this wreath—you can say I'm burlap obsessed! Burlap is so easy to work with and is such a versatile neutral color. I've paired it with my favorite ribbon pattern (buffalo plaid) and added vibrant burgundy fabric flowers to add a bright pop of autumn color. Weaving and folding the burlap is such a relaxing exercise for me that I can start this wreath while watching my favorite TV show or catching up on the day's news with my family.

BASIC SUPPLIES

- Glue gun
- Glue sticks
- Ribbon or cord for hanging

VARIATIONS

1. Add more of a country vibe to this wreath by adding a rustic sign or metal stars to the center.

2. Replace the 2 rolls of natural colored burlap with 2 rolls of burlap printed with a chevron pattern for a completely different look.

PROJECT SUPPLIES

- 14-inch wire wreath form
- 2 rolls of natural burlap, each 4 inches by 10 feet
- Fabric flowers in fall colors
- Fabric leaves and other foliage
- Tan pipe cleaners
- Wired decorative ribbon, 2-2½ inches wide by 8 feet long

Make your own decorative bow for this wreath. See Tutorial on page 110.

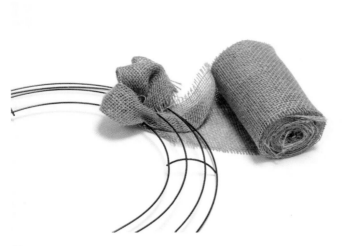

Figure 1

Figure 4

Figure 2

Figure 3

Start by tying the end of the burlap to the wire frame and continue weaving the burlap strip through the inner circle of the frame and working outward. Keep the weave loose. As you are weaving, each loop should be about 2 inches high. *Figures 1 & 2*

As you are weaving the burlap, secure small sections together with pipe cleaners to hold in place at the back of the form. Keep the sections as tight as possible so you will finish with a robust wreath. *Figure 3*

The goal is to make bubbles of burlap all around the form until it is full. *Figure 4*

Snip off loose strands of burlap. Keep any strands that you feel add to the natural beauty of the burlap. *Figure 5*

Before permanently affixing flowers, leaves, and ribbon, plan how you want to style your burlap wreath and trim down flowers and branches to fit. *Figure 6*

Affix leaves and flowers to burlap with a generous amount of glue. *Figures 7 & 8*

Attach ribbon or cord behind the wreath for hanging.

Figure 5

Figure 7

Figure 6

Figure 8

Welcome Pumpkin Door Hanging

For me, the official beginning of the holiday season starts in October. From the planning of Halloween costumes, carving of jack o' lanterns, fall decorating, pumpkin picking, and yes, even my birthday, this is a season of celebrating friends and family. When you're not outside in the crisp, autumn air, it's a great season for entertaining at home. I can almost smell the cinnamon in the apple pie baking in the oven! This pumpkin door hanging will provide a cheery welcome to all your visitors from early October through Thanksgiving.

BASIC SUPPLIES

- Floral wire, pipe cleaners, or tie wraps
- Glue gun
- Glue sticks
- Ribbon or cord for hanging
- Scissors

PROJECT SUPPLIES

- 14-inch wire wreath form
- Orange- or pumpkin-colored burlap
- Green burlap
- 2 small branches of fabric leaves with white berries
- A few strips of raffia
- Heavy-duty cotton ribbon, 2–2½ inches wide by 8 feet long
- 10–12-inch word sign in wood, metal, or fabric

Make your own decorative bow for this wreath. See Tutorial on page 110.

VARIATIONS

1. Use a different color burlap such as red to make an apple wreath. Use green burlap to make a leaf or two at the top of the apple.

2. Make a grouping of 3 pumpkin wall hangings, each with a different inspirational word, for example, "gather," "welcome," "family," "peace," etc.

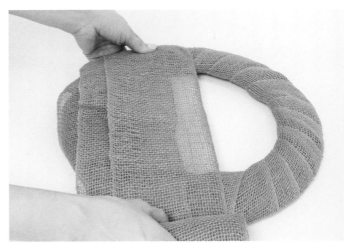

Figure 4

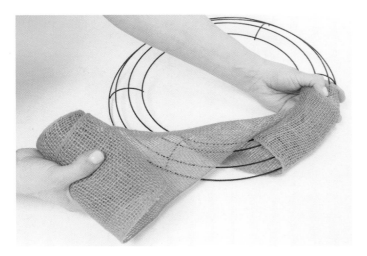

Figure 1

Figure 2

Figure 3

Starting on one side, begin to wrap the burlap around the wreath form. Use a little bit of glue on the burlap as you start to wrap to hold it in place for a few layers. As you continue wrapping, hold the burlap in place when needed with dabs of glue. *Figure 1*

Layer the burlap around the form until you have completed the circle. Cut the ribbon and glue down the end to secure. *Figure 2*

Fill in the pumpkin by wrapping the burlap from top to bottom several times. *Figures 3 & 4*

After you finish the wrapping to make the pumpkin, cut the burlap at the back of the wreath and glue the burlap down to the back of the form.

Use the green burlap to cut a couple of leaf shapes to place at the top of the pumpkin, and plan where you will place your word sign when you are ready to start securing the embellishments. *Figures 5 & 6*

Glue the center part of your burlap leaves, raffia, and fabric leaves to the top of the wreath to look like the top of the pumpkin. Make sure to keep the look loose and haphazard.

Glue your word sign to overlap the ribbon ends toward the center of the pumpkin. *Figure 7*

Attach ribbon or cord behind the wreath for hanging.

Figure 5

Figure 6

Figure 7

Rustic Wheel Wreath

My grandmother had an old white wagon wheel surrounded by flowers and plants outside her house, and I always loved sitting near it to do my summer reading. You can use any type of wheel to make this wreath, even an old bike wheel! That's what makes this project so unique—it's a beautiful wreath made in a creative way. Once again, being able to repurpose something old to create something new makes me happy.

BASIC SUPPLIES

- Floral wire, pipe cleaners, or tie wraps

- Glue

- Glue gun

- Wire cutters

PROJECT SUPPLIES

- Wagon wheel, any size, purchased or upcycled

- Chalk paint or stain of your choice

- 2 bunches of artificial fall flowers and leaves

- 3–4 branches of pussy willows

- Heavy-duty wreath hook or heavy-duty clips for hanging

VARIATIONS

1. Attach gourds as needed to add visual interest and bring in more fall flavor to this wreath.

2. Instead of hanging, rest this wheel near either a bush or a bench at the front of your house.

Figure 1

Figure 4

Figure 2

Paint or stain your wheel according to the manufacturer's instructions. *Figure 1*

Separate the pussy willow branches and snip off 8–12 stems to place around your wheel as a base. *Figure 2*

Glue the stems in place on the bottom half of the wheel, making sure the flowering ends fan out from the base. *Figures 3 & 4*

Use floral wire to attach the leaves to roughly half of the wagon wheel at the bottom. The leaves will be the base for the flowers.

After trimming off excess stems and leaves, affix flowers to the wagon wheel, toward the center of your leaf arrangement. *Figure 5*

Since this wreath will be heavy, use a heavy-duty or specialty wreath hook to support it or attach heavy-duty clips in a few places for hanging.

Figure 3

Figure 5

Pinecone Wreath

My Aunt Connie gifted me my very own pine tree when I was a little girl (I still have a photo of the happy event, see page 114). We planted it in our backyard that day. I must have done a fairly good job taking care of it (or nature was very helpful), because many years later I started to realize that my tree was growing and shedding pinecones. The pinecones would fall from my tree toward the end of summer, and I would collect them and proudly place them in a bowl on the dining room table. Because not everyone has their own pine tree, I used store-bought artificial pinecones for this project.

BASIC SUPPLIES

- Glue gun
- Glue sticks
- Ribbon or cord for hanging
- Scissors

PROJECT SUPPLIES

- 16-inch circular wooden wreath form
- White or cream craft paint and foam brush
- 4 dozen artificial pinecones in assorted sizes
- 12 long sprigs of fall branches with berries

VARIATIONS

1. Use bleached pinecones instead of natural pinecones or use spray paint to make the whole wreath the same color.

2. Cut the tips off of the pinecones and discard them. Paint the pinecones in rich jeweled colors. When they are dry, paint yellow dots at the bottom (widest part) of the painted pinecones to represent the center part of a flower. Glue the flat tops of the pinecones to the wreath form. You will have a wreath that looks like brightly colored dahlias.

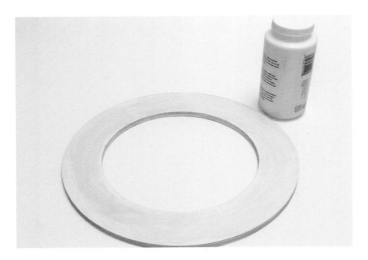

Figure 1

Figure 4

Start with a wooden wreath form and paint it white or cream. *Figure 1*

Prepare your pinecones as needed by making sure they are clean and by removing any loose pieces.

Glue the flat bottom of the first pinecone to the form. *Figure 2*

Starting next to the first pinecone, and making this the bottom of the wreath, select the best sizes of pinecones that will balance your wreath on both sides and glue them to the form. *Figure 3*

Continue gluing the pinecones to the circular form and to each other until the wreath is full of pinecones.

Plan how you will place your fall sprigs by interspersing them loosely in about a dozen spots around the wreath, having them fall out gracefully. *Figure 4*

When you are happy with how the sprigs are arranged, affix them to the wreath form and/or sides of the pinecones with glue.

Attach ribbon or cord behind the wreath for hanging.

Figure 2

Figure 3

DENIM ROSES
For the Recycled Paper Wreath
(see page 36)

Take any length of denim, cut the fabric, and then tear in about 2-inch strips. *Figures 1, 2 & 3*

Fold the denim strip in half on the short side; add a drop of glue inside at the end of the fabric. Fold the denim over to form a triangle. *Figures 4 & 5*

Secure the triangular part with glue. This will form the center of the rose. Twist the fabric away from you to start the petals. *Figures 6 & 7*

Continue to roll and twist the fabric as you wrap the fabric around the outside of the rose that is forming. Apply glue as you work to hold the petals together. *Figure 8*

If you allow the underside of the denim and rough edges to show, it will add a little more visual interest.

Figure 3

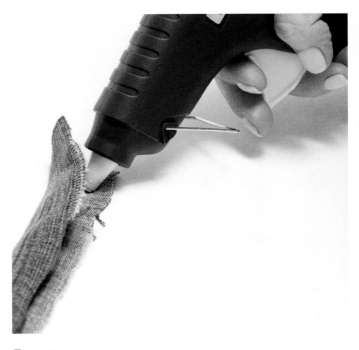

Figure 4

Figure 1

Figure 2

Figure 5

Figure 6

Figure 8

Figure 7

FELT FLOWERS
ROSES

For the Wire Hoop Wreath
(see page 28)

Cut out several circles of felt, some with 3-inch diameters, and some with 6-inch diameters. You can use the top of a glass or dish to make the circle shapes or copy and then trace the templates on page 107. *Figure 1*

Cut a spiral shape in a circular motion starting at the outermost edge of the spiral. *Figure 2*

Starting at the outermost part, add a drop of glue and roll the felt until you have used the entire piece. *Figure 3*

When you are finished rolling the flower, there will be a small flap at the end. Add a drop of glue and fold the flap over to secure. This will be the bottom of the flower. *Figure 4*

Figure 3

Figure 4

Figure 1

Figure 2

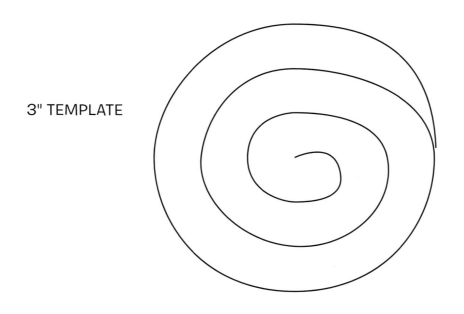

3" TEMPLATE

6" TEMPLATE

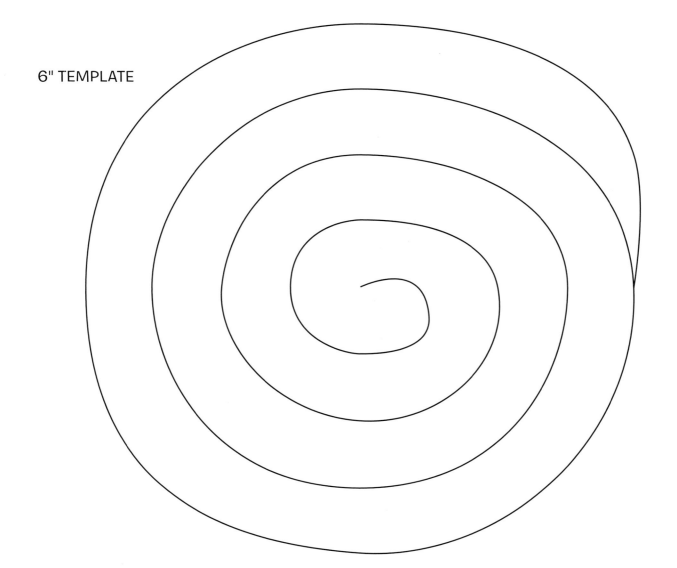

FELT FLOWERS
MUMS

For the Wire Hoop Wreath
(see page 28)

Cut a strip of felt about 10–12 inches long by 2–3 inches wide (the longer the strip, the wider the finished flower; the wider the strip, the taller the finished flower). *Figure 1*

Fold the strip in half. *Figure 2*

Snip the felt on the fold every ³⁄₈ inch from one end to the other. Make the snips about ¾ inch long. *Figure 3*

Add a small drop of glue at the first notch on the right side of the strip. *Figure 4*

Slowly roll the flower, adding a drop of glue when needed to hold the flower together. Brush your hand lightly across the top of the flower to fluff it. *Figure 5*

Use the template to cut out as many leaves as you will need.

Figure 3

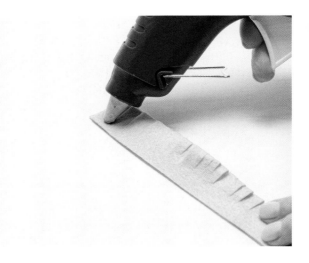

Figure 4

Figure 1

Figure 2

Figure 5

LEAF TEMPLATE

EASY BOW

Here is how to make an easy bow using 3 pieces of wired ribbon. My measurements here are just suggestions. Cut a 12-inch piece of ribbon and place it down on a table. Cut an 18-inch piece of ribbon and fold it roughly into thirds. Lay this piece on top of the 12-inch piece on your work surface. Lift both ribbons together and use a tie wrap to attach the two together at the center of both. Trim off the excess tie wrap after sealing it around the ribbon. *Figure 1*

To make it easy to attach the bow to a wreath, pull a pipe cleaner through the tie wrap at the center, twisting it tightly at the middle 2 or 3 times to make sure it's secure. Leaving the ends of the pipe cleaner uncovered, add a small drop of glue at the center of the tie wrap. Cut a small 2½-inch piece of ribbon and wrap it around the center to finish off the bow. *Figure 2*

Cut the tails at about a 45-degree angle or cut a "V" at each end. *Figure 3*

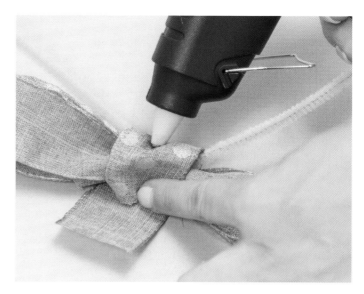

Figure 2

Figure 1

Figure 3

MY FAVORITE BOW

Wrap a length of wired ribbon about 2 yards long around 3 fingers of your non-dominant hand to form a circle that overlaps slightly. This is the center of your bow. *Figure 1*

Remove your fingers from the loop you just made and hold the center loosely. Fold the ribbon back under the loop you just made, creating another loop that extends about 2–2½ inches from the center loop. Fold back under the center loop and do the same thing on the other side. Pinch the ribbon securely between your fingers. *Figure 2*

Repeat this step 4 more times, extending each round by approximately a half inch. You should finish with 5 loops total on each side of the center of your bow. *Figure 3*

Feed a tie wrap through the center loop. Make sure that you capture all of the loops as you close the tie wrap. Trim off the excess tie wrap and secure with glue. *Figures 4 & 5*

To make it easy to attach the bow to a wreath, pull a pipe cleaner through the tie wrap at the center, twisting it tightly at the middle 2 or 3 times to make sure it's secure. *Figure 6*

Trim excess ribbon and puff up the loops to finish.

If you want your bow to have long tails, cut a 2-foot-long piece of ribbon off the spool with fabric scissors. Take the free end and pass it through the center loop of your bow so it covers the tie wrap (be sure to leave the pipe cleaner uncovered). Tie a basic knot at the middle, allowing the 2 ends of the ribbon to hang down. Cut the tails at about a 45-degree angle or cut a "V" at each end. *Figure 7*

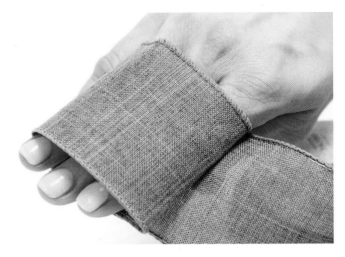

Figure 1

Figure 2

Figure 3

Figure 4

Figure 6

Figure 5

Figure 7

FIRECRACKER ROCKET
For the Fourth of July Rag Wreath
(see page 58)

For 2 firecracker rockets, you will need 2 empty toilet paper rolls and 2 squares of seasonal themed scrapbook paper. *Figure 1*

Lay your empty paper roll on top of one square of paper and trim it to the length of the roll. *Figure 2*

Use a small piece of tape to secure the paper to the roll, then wrap the paper around the roll so that it overlaps. Add another small piece of tape to secure it. (This tape will be hidden when you affix it to the wreath.) *Figures 3 & 4*

With another piece of scrapbook paper in a contrasting color, cut out a circle with a 3½-inch diameter. (If you don't have a compass, you can trace the top of a glass or dish with similar measurements.) *Figures 5 & 6*

Cut a slit halfway through the circle. *Figure 7*

Overlap the 2 end pieces slightly so that it forms a little cone; add a little glue to secure. *Figure 8*

Add a little glue to the top of one end of the decorated paper roll and attach the cone to complete your firecracker rocket. Embellish with glittery spirals. *Figure 9*

Figure 2

Figure 3

Figure 1

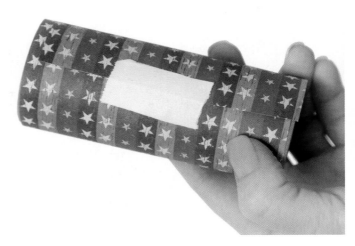

Figure 4

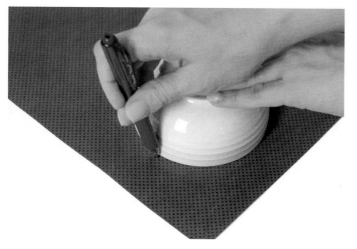

Figure 5

Figure 8

Figure 6

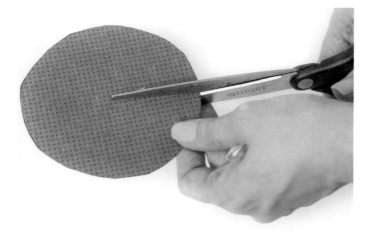

Figure 7

Figure 9

A young Stasie poses with a gift from her Aunt Connie—
a tree, which many years later would bear pinecones!
See Stasie's pinecone wreath on page 100.

About the Author

NEW YORK native Stasie McArthur is also the author of Dover's *Spa Apothecary*.
She has been making homemade and handmade gifts for friends and family for
more than 20 years. Stasie is skilled in a wide variety of crafts, from knitting and
crochet to refurbishing furniture and wreath-making, preparing natural remedies
and herbs, and cooking and baking.

View Stasie's work on Instagram @craftystasie and www.etsy.com/shop/craftystasieco.